MW01602118

homeschool
LESSON PLANNING
notebook

HOMESCHOOL YEAR:

52 WEEK UNDATED PLANNER

YOUR PLANNER INCLUDES

- BLANK GRID PAGES
- 12-MONTH CALENDAR
- FIELD TRIPS
- ATTENDANCE TRACKER
- CLASSES
- CURRICULUM OVERVIEW
- BOOK LIST
- CURRICULUM PROGRESS TRACKER

12 UNDATED MONTHLY CALENDAR PAGES

52 WEEKS OF:
- WEEKLY GOALS, NOTES, & SCHEDULE LAYOUT
- WEEKLY LESSON PLAN GRID
- DAILY DETAILS (6 PER WEEK)
- END OF WEEK REFLECTION
- END OF THE YEAR REFLECTION

schoolnest

ART + BOOKS + NATURE

SECOND EDITION

www.theschoolnest.com

CALENDAR

FIELD TRIPS

ATTENDANCE

												MONTH
1	1	1	1	1	1	1	1	1	1	1	1	
2	2	2	2	2	2	2	2	2	2	2	2	
3	3	3	3	3	3	3	3	3	3	3	3	
4	4	4	4	4	4	4	4	4	4	4	4	
5	5	5	5	5	5	5	5	5	5	5	5	
6	6	6	6	6	6	6	6	6	6	6	6	
7	7	7	7	7	7	7	7	7	7	7	7	
8	8	8	8	8	8	8	8	8	8	8	8	
9	9	9	9	9	9	9	9	9	9	9	9	
10	10	10	10	10	10	10	10	10	10	10	10	
11	11	11	11	11	11	11	11	11	11	11	11	
12	12	12	12	12	12	12	12	12	12	12	12	
13	13	13	13	13	13	13	13	13	13	13	13	
14	14	14	14	14	14	14	14	14	14	14	14	
15	15	15	15	15	15	15	15	15	15	15	15	
16	16	16	16	16	16	16	16	16	16	16	16	
17	17	17	17	17	17	17	17	17	17	17	17	
18	18	18	18	18	18	18	18	18	18	18	18	
19	19	19	19	19	19	19	19	19	19	19	19	
20	20	20	20	20	20	20	20	20	20	20	20	
21	21	21	21	21	21	21	21	21	21	21	21	
22	22	22	22	22	22	22	22	22	22	22	22	
23	23	23	23	23	23	23	23	23	23	23	23	
24	24	24	24	24	24	24	24	24	24	24	24	
25	25	25	25	25	25	25	25	25	25	25	25	
26	26	26	26	26	26	26	26	26	26	26	26	
27	27	27	27	27	27	27	27	27	27	27	27	
28	28	28	28	28	28	28	28	28	28	28	28	
29	29	29	29	29	29	29	29	29	29	29	29	
30	30	30	30	30	30	30	30	30	30	30	30	
31	31	31	31	31	31	31	31	31	31	31	31	
												TOTAL

CLASSES

CURRICULUM OVERVIEW

CURRICULUM OVERVIEW

CURRICULUM OVERVIEW

CURRICULUM OVERVIEW

CURRICULUM OVERVIEW

BOOK LIST

BOOK LIST

BOOK LIST

BOOK LIST

CURRICULUM PROGRESS

1	2	3	4	5	6	7	8	9	10	11	12	13	14	15	16	17	18	19	20
21	22	23	24	25	26	27	28	29	30	31	32	33	34	35	36	37	38	39	40
41	42	43	44	45	46	47	48	49	50	51	52	53	54	55	56	57	58	59	60
61	62	63	64	65	66	67	68	69	70	71	72	73	74	75	76	77	78	79	80
81	82	83	84	85	86	87	88	89	90	91	92	93	94	95	96	97	98	99	100
101	102	103	104	105	106	107	108	109	110	111	112	113	114	115	116	117	118	119	120
121	122	123	124	125	126	127	128	129	130	131	132	133	134	135	136	137	138	139	140
141	142	143	144	145	146	147	148	149	150	151	152	153	154	155	156	157	158	159	160
161	162	163	164	165	166	167	168	169	170	171	172	173	174	175	176	177	178	179	180

1	2	3	4	5	6	7	8	9	10	11	12	13	14	15	16	17	18	19	20
21	22	23	24	25	26	27	28	29	30	31	32	33	34	35	36	37	38	39	40
41	42	43	44	45	46	47	48	49	50	51	52	53	54	55	56	57	58	59	60
61	62	63	64	65	66	67	68	69	70	71	72	73	74	75	76	77	78	79	80
81	82	83	84	85	86	87	88	89	90	91	92	93	94	95	96	97	98	99	100
101	102	103	104	105	106	107	108	109	110	111	112	113	114	115	116	117	118	119	120
121	122	123	124	125	126	127	128	129	130	131	132	133	134	135	136	137	138	139	140
141	142	143	144	145	146	147	148	149	150	151	152	153	154	155	156	157	158	159	160
161	162	163	164	165	166	167	168	169	170	171	172	173	174	175	176	177	178	179	180

1	2	3	4	5	6	7	8	9	10	11	12	13	14	15	16	17	18	19	20
21	22	23	24	25	26	27	28	29	30	31	32	33	34	35	36	37	38	39	40
41	42	43	44	45	46	47	48	49	50	51	52	53	54	55	56	57	58	59	60
61	62	63	64	65	66	67	68	69	70	71	72	73	74	75	76	77	78	79	80
81	82	83	84	85	86	87	88	89	90	91	92	93	94	95	96	97	98	99	100
101	102	103	104	105	106	107	108	109	110	111	112	113	114	115	116	117	118	119	120
121	122	123	124	125	126	127	128	129	130	131	132	133	134	135	136	137	138	139	140
141	142	143	144	145	146	147	148	149	150	151	152	153	154	155	156	157	158	159	160
161	162	163	164	165	166	167	168	169	170	171	172	173	174	175	176	177	178	179	180

CURRICULUM PROGRESS

1	2	3	4	5	6	7	8	9	10	11	12	13	14	15	16	17	18	19	20
21	22	23	24	25	26	27	28	29	30	31	32	33	34	35	36	37	38	39	40
41	42	43	44	45	46	47	48	49	50	51	52	53	54	55	56	57	58	59	60
61	62	63	64	65	66	67	68	69	70	71	72	73	74	75	76	77	78	79	80
81	82	83	84	85	86	87	88	89	90	91	92	93	94	95	96	97	98	99	100
101	102	103	104	105	106	107	108	109	110	111	112	113	114	115	116	117	118	119	120
121	122	123	124	125	126	127	128	129	130	131	132	133	134	135	136	137	138	139	140
141	142	143	144	145	146	147	148	149	150	151	152	153	154	155	156	157	158	159	160
161	162	163	164	165	166	167	168	169	170	171	172	173	174	175	176	177	178	179	180

1	2	3	4	5	6	7	8	9	10	11	12	13	14	15	16	17	18	19	20
21	22	23	24	25	26	27	28	29	30	31	32	33	34	35	36	37	38	39	40
41	42	43	44	45	46	47	48	49	50	51	52	53	54	55	56	57	58	59	60
61	62	63	64	65	66	67	68	69	70	71	72	73	74	75	76	77	78	79	80
81	82	83	84	85	86	87	88	89	90	91	92	93	94	95	96	97	98	99	100
101	102	103	104	105	106	107	108	109	110	111	112	113	114	115	116	117	118	119	120
121	122	123	124	125	126	127	128	129	130	131	132	133	134	135	136	137	138	139	140
141	142	143	144	145	146	147	148	149	150	151	152	153	154	155	156	157	158	159	160
161	162	163	164	165	166	167	168	169	170	171	172	173	174	175	176	177	178	179	180

1	2	3	4	5	6	7	8	9	10	11	12	13	14	15	16	17	18	19	20
21	22	23	24	25	26	27	28	29	30	31	32	33	34	35	36	37	38	39	40
41	42	43	44	45	46	47	48	49	50	51	52	53	54	55	56	57	58	59	60
61	62	63	64	65	66	67	68	69	70	71	72	73	74	75	76	77	78	79	80
81	82	83	84	85	86	87	88	89	90	91	92	93	94	95	96	97	98	99	100
101	102	103	104	105	106	107	108	109	110	111	112	113	114	115	116	117	118	119	120
121	122	123	124	125	126	127	128	129	130	131	132	133	134	135	136	137	138	139	140
141	142	143	144	145	146	147	148	149	150	151	152	153	154	155	156	157	158	159	160
161	162	163	164	165	166	167	168	169	170	171	172	173	174	175	176	177	178	179	180

CURRICULUM PROGRESS

1	2	3	4	5	6	7	8	9	10	11	12	13	14	15	16	17	18	19	20
21	22	23	24	25	26	27	28	29	30	31	32	33	34	35	36	37	38	39	40
41	42	43	44	45	46	47	48	49	50	51	52	53	54	55	56	57	58	59	60
61	62	63	64	65	66	67	68	69	70	71	72	73	74	75	76	77	78	79	80
81	82	83	84	85	86	87	88	89	90	91	92	93	94	95	96	97	98	99	100
101	102	103	104	105	106	107	108	109	110	111	112	113	114	115	116	117	118	119	120
121	122	123	124	125	126	127	128	129	130	131	132	133	134	135	136	137	138	139	140
141	142	143	144	145	146	147	148	149	150	151	152	153	154	155	156	157	158	159	160
161	162	163	164	165	166	167	168	169	170	171	172	173	174	175	176	177	178	179	180

1	2	3	4	5	6	7	8	9	10	11	12	13	14	15	16	17	18	19	20
21	22	23	24	25	26	27	28	29	30	31	32	33	34	35	36	37	38	39	40
41	42	43	44	45	46	47	48	49	50	51	52	53	54	55	56	57	58	59	60
61	62	63	64	65	66	67	68	69	70	71	72	73	74	75	76	77	78	79	80
81	82	83	84	85	86	87	88	89	90	91	92	93	94	95	96	97	98	99	100
101	102	103	104	105	106	107	108	109	110	111	112	113	114	115	116	117	118	119	120
121	122	123	124	125	126	127	128	129	130	131	132	133	134	135	136	137	138	139	140
141	142	143	144	145	146	147	148	149	150	151	152	153	154	155	156	157	158	159	160
161	162	163	164	165	166	167	168	169	170	171	172	173	174	175	176	177	178	179	180

1	2	3	4	5	6	7	8	9	10	11	12	13	14	15	16	17	18	19	20
21	22	23	24	25	26	27	28	29	30	31	32	33	34	35	36	37	38	39	40
41	42	43	44	45	46	47	48	49	50	51	52	53	54	55	56	57	58	59	60
61	62	63	64	65	66	67	68	69	70	71	72	73	74	75	76	77	78	79	80
81	82	83	84	85	86	87	88	89	90	91	92	93	94	95	96	97	98	99	100
101	102	103	104	105	106	107	108	109	110	111	112	113	114	115	116	117	118	119	120
121	122	123	124	125	126	127	128	129	130	131	132	133	134	135	136	137	138	139	140
141	142	143	144	145	146	147	148	149	150	151	152	153	154	155	156	157	158	159	160
161	162	163	164	165	166	167	168	169	170	171	172	173	174	175	176	177	178	179	180

CURRICULUM PROGRESS

1	2	3	4	5	6	7	8	9	10	11	12	13	14	15	16	17	18	19	20
21	22	23	24	25	26	27	28	29	30	31	32	33	34	35	36	37	38	39	40
41	42	43	44	45	46	47	48	49	50	51	52	53	54	55	56	57	58	59	60
61	62	63	64	65	66	67	68	69	70	71	72	73	74	75	76	77	78	79	80
81	82	83	84	85	86	87	88	89	90	91	92	93	94	95	96	97	98	99	100
101	102	103	104	105	106	107	108	109	110	111	112	113	114	115	116	117	118	119	120
121	122	123	124	125	126	127	128	129	130	131	132	133	134	135	136	137	138	139	140
141	142	143	144	145	146	147	148	149	150	151	152	153	154	155	156	157	158	159	160
161	162	163	164	165	166	167	168	169	170	171	172	173	174	175	176	177	178	179	180

1	2	3	4	5	6	7	8	9	10	11	12	13	14	15	16	17	18	19	20
21	22	23	24	25	26	27	28	29	30	31	32	33	34	35	36	37	38	39	40
41	42	43	44	45	46	47	48	49	50	51	52	53	54	55	56	57	58	59	60
61	62	63	64	65	66	67	68	69	70	71	72	73	74	75	76	77	78	79	80
81	82	83	84	85	86	87	88	89	90	91	92	93	94	95	96	97	98	99	100
101	102	103	104	105	106	107	108	109	110	111	112	113	114	115	116	117	118	119	120
121	122	123	124	125	126	127	128	129	130	131	132	133	134	135	136	137	138	139	140
141	142	143	144	145	146	147	148	149	150	151	152	153	154	155	156	157	158	159	160
161	162	163	164	165	166	167	168	169	170	171	172	173	174	175	176	177	178	179	180

1	2	3	4	5	6	7	8	9	10	11	12	13	14	15	16	17	18	19	20
21	22	23	24	25	26	27	28	29	30	31	32	33	34	35	36	37	38	39	40
41	42	43	44	45	46	47	48	49	50	51	52	53	54	55	56	57	58	59	60
61	62	63	64	65	66	67	68	69	70	71	72	73	74	75	76	77	78	79	80
81	82	83	84	85	86	87	88	89	90	91	92	93	94	95	96	97	98	99	100
101	102	103	104	105	106	107	108	109	110	111	112	113	114	115	116	117	118	119	120
121	122	123	124	125	126	127	128	129	130	131	132	133	134	135	136	137	138	139	140
141	142	143	144	145	146	147	148	149	150	151	152	153	154	155	156	157	158	159	160
161	162	163	164	165	166	167	168	169	170	171	172	173	174	175	176	177	178	179	180

MONTH OF

MONTH OF

MONTH OF

MONTH OF

MONTH OF

MONTH OF

MONTH OF

MONTH OF

MONTH OF

MONTH OF

MONTH OF

MONTH OF

This Week

WEEKLY GOALS & NOTES

SCHEDULE

WEEKLY PLAN

WEEKLY PLAN

DAILY DETAILS

DAILY DETAILS

DAILY DETAILS

WEEKLY REFLECTIONS

This Week

WEEKLY GOALS & NOTES

SCHEDULE

WEEKLY PLAN

WEEKLY PLAN

DAILY DETAILS

DAILY DETAILS

DAILY DETAILS

WEEKLY REFLECTIONS

This Week

WEEKLY GOALS & NOTES

SCHEDULE

WEEKLY PLAN

WEEKLY PLAN

DAILY DETAILS

DAILY DETAILS

DAILY DETAILS

WEEKLY REFLECTIONS

This Week

WEEKLY GOALS & NOTES

SCHEDULE

WEEKLY PLAN

WEEKLY PLAN

DAILY DETAILS

DAILY DETAILS

DAILY DETAILS

WEEKLY REFLECTIONS

This Week

WEEKLY GOALS & NOTES

SCHEDULE

WEEKLY PLAN

WEEKLY PLAN

DAILY DETAILS

DAILY DETAILS

DAILY DETAILS

WEEKLY REFLECTIONS

This Week

WEEKLY GOALS & NOTES

SCHEDULE

WEEKLY PLAN

WEEKLY PLAN

DAILY DETAILS

DAILY DETAILS

DAILY DETAILS

WEEKLY REFLECTIONS

This Week

WEEKLY GOALS
& NOTES

SCHEDULE

WEEKLY PLAN

WEEKLY PLAN

DAILY DETAILS

DAILY DETAILS

DAILY DETAILS

WEEKLY REFLECTIONS

This Week

WEEKLY GOALS & NOTES

SCHEDULE

WEEKLY PLAN

WEEKLY PLAN

DAILY DETAILS

DAILY DETAILS

DAILY DETAILS

WEEKLY REFLECTIONS

This Week

WEEKLY GOALS & NOTES

SCHEDULE

WEEKLY PLAN

WEEKLY PLAN

DAILY DETAILS

DAILY DETAILS

DAILY DETAILS

WEEKLY REFLECTIONS

This Week

WEEKLY GOALS & NOTES

SCHEDULE

WEEKLY PLAN

WEEKLY PLAN

DAILY DETAILS

DAILY DETAILS

DAILY DETAILS

WEEKLY REFLECTIONS

This Week

WEEKLY GOALS & NOTES

SCHEDULE

WEEKLY PLAN

WEEKLY PLAN

DAILY DETAILS

DAILY DETAILS

DAILY DETAILS

WEEKLY REFLECTIONS

This Week

WEEKLY GOALS & NOTES

SCHEDULE

WEEKLY PLAN

WEEKLY PLAN

DAILY DETAILS

DAILY DETAILS

DAILY DETAILS

WEEKLY REFLECTIONS

This Week

WEEKLY GOALS & NOTES

SCHEDULE

WEEKLY PLAN

WEEKLY PLAN

DAILY DETAILS

DAILY DETAILS

DAILY DETAILS

WEEKLY REFLECTIONS

This Week

WEEKLY GOALS & NOTES

SCHEDULE

WEEKLY PLAN

WEEKLY PLAN

DAILY DETAILS

DAILY DETAILS

DAILY DETAILS

WEEKLY REFLECTIONS

This Week

WEEKLY GOALS & NOTES

SCHEDULE

WEEKLY PLAN

WEEKLY PLAN

DAILY DETAILS

DAILY DETAILS

DAILY DETAILS

WEEKLY REFLECTIONS

This Week

WEEKLY GOALS & NOTES

SCHEDULE

WEEKLY PLAN

WEEKLY PLAN

DAILY DETAILS

DAILY DETAILS

DAILY DETAILS

WEEKLY REFLECTIONS

This Week

WEEKLY GOALS & NOTES

SCHEDULE

WEEKLY PLAN

WEEKLY PLAN

DAILY DETAILS

DAILY DETAILS

DAILY DETAILS

WEEKLY REFLECTIONS

This Week

WEEKLY GOALS & NOTES

SCHEDULE

WEEKLY PLAN

WEEKLY PLAN

DAILY DETAILS

DAILY DETAILS

DAILY DETAILS

WEEKLY REFLECTIONS

This Week

WEEKLY GOALS & NOTES

SCHEDULE

WEEKLY PLAN

WEEKLY PLAN

DAILY DETAILS

DAILY DETAILS

DAILY DETAILS

WEEKLY REFLECTIONS

This Week

WEEKLY GOALS & NOTES

SCHEDULE

WEEKLY PLAN

WEEKLY PLAN

DAILY DETAILS

DAILY DETAILS

DAILY DETAILS

WEEKLY REFLECTIONS

This Week

WEEKLY GOALS & NOTES

SCHEDULE

WEEKLY PLAN

WEEKLY PLAN

DAILY DETAILS

DAILY DETAILS

DAILY DETAILS

WEEKLY REFLECTIONS

This Week

WEEKLY GOALS & NOTES

SCHEDULE

WEEKLY PLAN

WEEKLY PLAN

DAILY DETAILS

DAILY DETAILS

DAILY DETAILS

WEEKLY REFLECTIONS

This Week

WEEKLY GOALS & NOTES

SCHEDULE

WEEKLY PLAN

WEEKLY PLAN

DAILY DETAILS

DAILY DETAILS

DAILY DETAILS

WEEKLY REFLECTIONS

This Week

WEEKLY GOALS & NOTES

SCHEDULE

WEEKLY PLAN

WEEKLY PLAN

DAILY DETAILS

DAILY DETAILS

DAILY DETAILS

WEEKLY REFLECTIONS

This Week

WEEKLY GOALS & NOTES

SCHEDULE

WEEKLY PLAN

WEEKLY PLAN

DAILY DETAILS

DAILY DETAILS

DAILY DETAILS

WEEKLY REFLECTIONS

This Week

WEEKLY GOALS & NOTES

SCHEDULE

WEEKLY PLAN

WEEKLY PLAN

DAILY DETAILS

DAILY DETAILS

DAILY DETAILS

WEEKLY REFLECTIONS

This Week

WEEKLY GOALS & NOTES

SCHEDULE

WEEKLY PLAN

WEEKLY PLAN

DAILY DETAILS

DAILY DETAILS

DAILY DETAILS

WEEKLY REFLECTIONS

This Week

WEEKLY GOALS
& NOTES

SCHEDULE

WEEKLY PLAN

WEEKLY PLAN

DAILY DETAILS

DAILY DETAILS

DAILY DETAILS

WEEKLY REFLECTIONS

This Week

WEEKLY GOALS & NOTES

SCHEDULE

WEEKLY PLAN

WEEKLY PLAN

DAILY DETAILS

DAILY DETAILS

DAILY DETAILS

WEEKLY REFLECTIONS

This Week

WEEKLY GOALS & NOTES

SCHEDULE

WEEKLY PLAN

WEEKLY PLAN

DAILY DETAILS

DAILY DETAILS

DAILY DETAILS

WEEKLY REFLECTIONS

This Week

WEEKLY GOALS & NOTES

SCHEDULE

WEEKLY PLAN

WEEKLY PLAN

DAILY DETAILS

DAILY DETAILS

DAILY DETAILS

WEEKLY REFLECTIONS

This Week

WEEKLY GOALS & NOTES

SCHEDULE

WEEKLY PLAN

WEEKLY PLAN

DAILY DETAILS

DAILY DETAILS

DAILY DETAILS

WEEKLY REFLECTIONS

This Week

WEEKLY GOALS & NOTES

SCHEDULE

WEEKLY PLAN

WEEKLY PLAN

DAILY DETAILS

DAILY DETAILS

DAILY DETAILS

WEEKLY REFLECTIONS

This Week

WEEKLY GOALS & NOTES

SCHEDULE

WEEKLY PLAN

WEEKLY PLAN

DAILY DETAILS

DAILY DETAILS

DAILY DETAILS

WEEKLY REFLECTIONS

This Week

WEEKLY GOALS & NOTES

SCHEDULE

WEEKLY PLAN

WEEKLY PLAN

DAILY DETAILS

DAILY DETAILS

DAILY DETAILS

WEEKLY REFLECTIONS

This Week

WEEKLY GOALS & NOTES

SCHEDULE

WEEKLY PLAN

WEEKLY PLAN

DAILY DETAILS

DAILY DETAILS

DAILY DETAILS

WEEKLY REFLECTIONS

This Week

WEEKLY GOALS & NOTES

SCHEDULE

WEEKLY PLAN

WEEKLY PLAN

DAILY DETAILS

DAILY DETAILS

DAILY DETAILS

WEEKLY REFLECTIONS

This Week

WEEKLY GOALS & NOTES

SCHEDULE

WEEKLY PLAN

WEEKLY PLAN

DAILY DETAILS

DAILY DETAILS

DAILY DETAILS

WEEKLY REFLECTIONS

This Week

WEEKLY GOALS & NOTES

SCHEDULE

WEEKLY PLAN

WEEKLY PLAN

DAILY DETAILS

DAILY DETAILS

DAILY DETAILS

WEEKLY REFLECTIONS

This Week

WEEKLY GOALS & NOTES

SCHEDULE

WEEKLY PLAN

WEEKLY PLAN

DAILY DETAILS

DAILY DETAILS

DAILY DETAILS

WEEKLY REFLECTIONS

This Week

WEEKLY GOALS & NOTES

SCHEDULE

WEEKLY PLAN

WEEKLY PLAN

DAILY DETAILS

DAILY DETAILS

DAILY DETAILS

WEEKLY REFLECTIONS

This Week

WEEKLY GOALS & NOTES

SCHEDULE

WEEKLY PLAN

WEEKLY PLAN

DAILY DETAILS

DAILY DETAILS

DAILY DETAILS

WEEKLY REFLECTIONS

This Week

WEEKLY GOALS & NOTES

WEEKLY PLAN

WEEKLY PLAN

DAILY DETAILS

DAILY DETAILS

DAILY DETAILS

WEEKLY REFLECTIONS

This Week

WEEKLY GOALS
& NOTES

SCHEDULE

WEEKLY PLAN

WEEKLY PLAN

DAILY DETAILS

DAILY DETAILS

DAILY DETAILS

WEEKLY REFLECTIONS

This Week

WEEKLY GOALS & NOTES

SCHEDULE

WEEKLY PLAN

WEEKLY PLAN

DAILY DETAILS

DAILY DETAILS

DAILY DETAILS

WEEKLY REFLECTIONS

This Week

WEEKLY GOALS & NOTES

SCHEDULE

WEEKLY PLAN

WEEKLY PLAN

DAILY DETAILS

DAILY DETAILS

DAILY DETAILS

WEEKLY REFLECTIONS

This Week

WEEKLY GOALS & NOTES

SCHEDULE

WEEKLY PLAN

WEEKLY PLAN

DAILY DETAILS

DAILY DETAILS

DAILY DETAILS

WEEKLY REFLECTIONS

This Week

WEEKLY GOALS & NOTES

SCHEDULE

WEEKLY PLAN

WEEKLY PLAN

DAILY DETAILS

DAILY DETAILS

DAILY DETAILS

WEEKLY REFLECTIONS

This Week

WEEKLY GOALS
& NOTES

SCHEDULE

WEEKLY PLAN

WEEKLY PLAN

DAILY DETAILS

DAILY DETAILS

DAILY DETAILS

WEEKLY REFLECTIONS

This Week

WEEKLY GOALS & NOTES

SCHEDULE

WEEKLY PLAN

WEEKLY PLAN

DAILY DETAILS

DAILY DETAILS

DAILY DETAILS

WEEKLY REFLECTIONS

This Week

WEEKLY GOALS & NOTES

SCHEDULE

WEEKLY PLAN

WEEKLY PLAN

DAILY DETAILS

DAILY DETAILS

DAILY DETAILS

WEEKLY REFLECTIONS

This Week

WEEKLY GOALS & NOTES

SCHEDULE

WEEKLY PLAN

WEEKLY PLAN

DAILY DETAILS

DAILY DETAILS

DAILY DETAILS

WEEKLY REFLECTIONS

END OF THE YEAR WRAP-UP

WHAT WENT WELL:

FOCUS FOR NEXT YEAR:

END OF THE YEAR WRAP-UP

WHAT WENT WELL:

FOCUS FOR NEXT YEAR:

Made in United States
Orlando, FL
30 June 2025

62543098R00256